Allison Emery Drake

The authorship of the West Saxon gospels

Allison Emery Drake

The authorship of the West Saxon gospels

ISBN/EAN: 9783337282493

Printed in Europe, USA, Canada, Australia, Japan

Cover: Foto ©Thomas Meinert / pixelio.de

More available books at **www.hansebooks.com**

THE AUTHORSHIP OF
THE WEST SAXON GOSPELS

BY

ALLISON DRAKE, A. M., Ph.D.,

UNIVERSITY FELLOW IN ANGLO-SAXON
IN COLUMBIA COLLEGE

NEW YORK
1894

Henrico Thurstoni Peck, Ph.D., L.H.D.,

Viro Eruditissimo Atque Acutissimo,

Professori Linguae Latinae Litterarumque

In Collegio Columbiae Neo-Eboracensi,

Pietatis Testimonium.

PREFATORY NOTE.

I wish to take this opportunity to express my sincere thanks for the kindly encouragement and valuable suggestions given me from the first by my instructor in Latin, Professor H. T. Peck, to whom alone until all the data were collected I communicated the nature of this work. I am greatly indebted to my instructor in Anglo-Saxon, Professor A. V. W. Jackson, who, by his zealous and quickening instruction and by his generous and unstinted assistance in revising the work for publication, has contributed much of whatever merits it possesses. My instructor, Professor T. R. Price, of the Department of English, has contributed some felicitous criticisms. These acknowledgments, however, should not make anyone but myself answerable for the shortcomings of this paper.

Although my other instructors, Professor A. C. Merriam, of the Department of Greek Archæology and Epigraphy, Professor E. D. Perry, of the Department of Sanskrit and Classical Philology, and Professor Brander Matthews, of the Department of Literature, have only indirectly influenced the production of this dissertation, I cannot refrain from expressing my high appreciation of their kindness and courtesy and the inspiration of their instruction.

A. D.

COLUMBIA COLLEGE, May 28, 1894.

CONTENTS.

	PAGE
Chief Works Used or Consulted	9
Introduction	11
The Anglo-Saxon Gospels	11
A. The Manuscripts	11
B. The Printed Editions	14
The Authorship of the West Saxon Gospels	17
The Evidence of Composite Authorship	22
i. Heofon, Heofone	23
ii. Underfon, Onfon	25
iii. þæt He Wolde, etc.	27
iv. þæra, Þara, etc.	31
v. Witodlice	34
vi. Hana, Cocc	35
vii. Stridor Dentium	36
viii. Fulgor	36
ix. Centurio	36
x. Vox Clamantis	37
xi. Uppan (On-uppan)	37
xii. Trado: Belæwan, (Ge)syllan	40
Résumé	44

CHIEF WORKS USED OR CONSULTED.

The Holy Gospels in Anglo-Saxon, Northumbrian and Old Mercian versions. W. W. Skeat, Cambridge, 1871-1887. (This work is the basis of the present dissertation).

Biblia Sacra Juxta Vulgatæ Exemplaria et Correctoria Romana. A. C. Fillion. Imprimatur: + Joseph Arch. Lugdun. Parisiis, 1887.

The New Testament in the Original Greek. B. F. Westcott and F. J. A. Hort. New York, 1890.

Friedrich Ludwig Stamm's Ulfilas. Moritz Heyne. Achte Auflage. Paderborn und Münster, 1885.

The Gospel of Saint Luke in Anglo-Saxon. J. W. Bright. Oxford, 1893.

An Anglo-Saxon Dictionary. A—— Swiðrian. Joseph Bosworth; T. Northcote Toller. Oxford, 1882-1892. (Cited: B. & T.).

An Old English Grammar. E. Sievers. Albert S. Cook. Second Edition. Boston, 1887. (Cited: Cook's Sievers).

The Blickling Homilies of the Tenth Century. 3 vols. R Morris. London, 1874-1880. (Cited: Blick. Homl.).

Ælfric's Lives of Saints. 2 vols. W. W. Skeat. London, 1881, 1885. (Only the first volume used. Cited: Sk. Ælf. I).

The Homilies of the Anglo-Saxon Church. 2 vols. Benjamin Thorpe. London, 1844, 1846. (Cited: Th. Ælf. I, II).

A(e)lfrik de vetere et novo testamento, Pentateuch, Iosua, Buch der Richter und Hiob. C. W. M. Grein. Cassel and Goettingen, 1872. (Cited: Grein's Ælf.).

The Oldest English Texts. Henry Sweet. London, 1885.

King Alfred's Orosius. Part I. Henry Sweet. London, 1883. (Cited: Sw. Alf. Oros.).

King Alfred's West-Saxon Version of Gregory's Pastoral Care. Henry Sweet. London, 1871. (Cited: Sw. Alf. C. P.).

Sancti Gregorii Papæ I, Cognomento Magni, Opera Omnia. Tomus Tertius. Patrologiæ Latinæ Tomus LXXVII. J.-P. Migne. Parisiis, 1862.

INTRODUCTION.

THE ANGLO-SAXON GOSPELS.

After careful investigation and consideration, Professor Skeat is inclined to the belief that West Saxon literature never possessed more than one version of the Gospels, and that that was made in the latter half of the tenth century (cf. Skeat's Pref. to Jn., p. vii; Pref. to Lk., p. xi). Besides this West Saxon version, there are also a Northumbrian gloss of all the Gospels, a modified form of that gloss for Mark, Luke and John, and an Old Mercian version of Matthew (cf. Skeat's Pref. to Jn., pp. xii, xiii ; Pref. to Mt., p. vii).

A. THE MANUSCRIPTS.

The following remarks about the MSS. and the printed editions of the Anglo-Saxon Gospels, down to printed edition no. IX, have been copied from Professor Skeat's Prefaces to the Gospels, often verbatim; but a verbatim transcript has not always been suitable for use in this brief paper. I have preferred to use the term *West Saxon Gospels* instead of the less definite term *Anglo-Saxon Gospels*, when only the West Saxon version has had to be designated. Of course, in quoting the exact title of a printed edition, the substitution has not been made.

There have come down to us only the following eight MSS. of the Anglo-Saxon Gospels. Each of the first six contains the West Saxon version in whole or in part.

I.—(Cf. Skeat's Pref. to Mk., p. v). The Corpus MS.—MS. no. CXL (formerly S. 4) in the Library of Corpus Christi College, Cambridge. Its contents are the four Gospels in West Saxon, and some other documents, [notably] a homily, inserted between Mark and Luke. The homily begins—M (e n) þ a l (e o f e s t a n). Her onginð þ (æt) halie g (e) writ þe co(m) fra(m) hcofenan into hierusale(m). It ends—and se þe underfehð witigan on þæs witigan naman he underfehð þæs witigan mede. At the end of Matthew is this note: Ego Ælfricus scripsi hunc librum in Monasterio Baðþonio et dedi Brihtwoldo preposito. Ælfric did not write the whole of the Gospels; for a different hand wrote from the word *gorst-beam* (Mk. 12: 26) to *he* (Mk. 12: 38), which makes a page of the MS.

II.—(Cf. Skeat's Pref. to Mk., pp. vi, vii). The Cambridge MS. —MS. Ii. 2 11, in the Cambridge University Library. In 1566 it became the property of Matthew Parker, Archbishop of Canterbury, who gave it in 1574 to the University of Cambridge.

III.—(Cf. Skeat's Pref. to Mk., p. vii). The Bodley MS.— MS. Bodley NE. F. 3.15, now Bodley 441. Several leaves of the original MS. were lost, but all but one of them have since been "restored." The "restored" portions are Mk. 1: 1 to 4: 37; Mk. 16: 14 to the end of Mark; Lk. 24: 51 to the end of the Gospel (but cf. Skeat's note *ad loc.*); and Jn. 20: 9 nearly to the end (cf. Skeat's note *ad loc.*).

IV.—(Cf. Skeat's Pref. to Mk., p. viii). The Cotton MS.— MS. Cotton Otho C. 1, in the British Museum. Before the great fire of 1731, this MS. was defective only as far as Mt. 27: 6; but after the fire it was long thought to be only a charred mass. Sir Frederic Madden uniquely mounted even the smallest fragments and thus rendered them accessible to the public. The date of the Corpus, Bodley, and Cotton MSS. is supposed to belong to the last decade of the tenth century. The Cambridge MS. is thought to be of later date, probably about 1050.

V.—(Cf. Skeat's Pref. to Mk., p. x). The Hatton MS.—This MS., formerly marked Hatton 65, is now marked Hatton 38, and is in the Bodleian Library at Oxford. It once belonged to Rev. John Parker, son to the Archbishop. Mr. Parker "restored" a missing leaf (Luke 16). The MS. was written about the time of Henry II. It is interesting as showing how the language began to lose strength in its inflectional forms.

VI.—(Cf. id., ib.). The Royal MS.—This MS. is now in the Royal Library at the British Museum, where its class mark is

Bibl. Reg. 1 A. xiv. The MS. was probably written in the time of Stephen. The general agreement of the Hatton MS. with it is very close, excepting that the Royal MS. preserves more archaic forms. The Hatton MS. was copied from it. The last seven verses of Mark in the Royal MS. are in the handwriting of the Hatton scribe, which proves that the scribe of the Hatton MS. had access to some other MS. besides the Royal. The Royal MS. was copied from the Bodley (cf. Skeat's Pref. to Lk., p. viii). The pedigree of these six MSS. may be indicated thus (cf. Skeat's Pref. to Jn., p. vii):

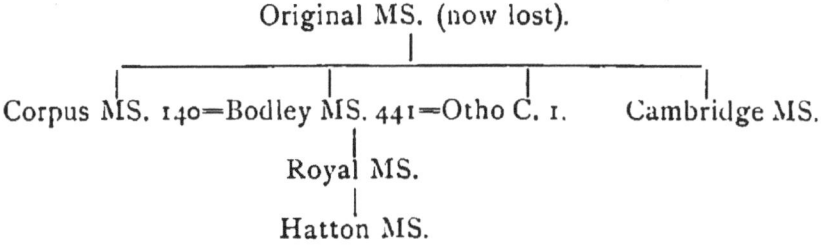

Original MS. (now lost).

Corpus MS. 140=Bodley MS. 441=Otho C. 1. Cambridge MS.

Royal MS.

Hatton MS.

VII.—(Cf. Skeat's Pref. to Mk., p. xi). The Lindisfarne MS.—This MS. is also known as the Durham Book. It is now one of the Cotton MSS. in the British Museum, its class mark being Nero D. 4. It contains the four Gospels in Latin, written in double columns, with an interlinear Northumbrian gloss. The Latin was written by Eadfrith in the island of Lindisfarne about A. D. 700. The gloss was written probably in the latter half of the tenth century, and exhibits two handwritings and two kinds of ink, one of the latter being red. The red ink and the second handwriting begin near the end of John 5: 10. This portion of the gloss is supposed to have been written by the glossator himself, Aldred, a priest; the previous portion having been made under his superintendence (cf. Skeat's Pref. to Jn., pp. viii, ff.).

VIII.—(Cf. Skeat's Pref. to Mk., pp. xii, xiii). The Rushworth MS.—This MS. is in the Bodleian Library at Oxford, and is marked Auct. D. ii. 19. The Latin is in single column and of uncertain date. The Anglo-Saxon of Matthew is a version in the Old Mercian dialect by Farman, a priest of Harewood, who is shown by the handwriting to have glossed the Mark as far as *hleonadun* in Mk. 2: 15, and to have translated John 18: 1-3. The remaining portion of the gloss was made by Owun, another inmate of Harewood. Dr. Murray observes that "the two portions of the gloss are contemporary, and owe their differences [dialectic?] to the different nativity of their writers" (cf. Skeat's Pref. to Jn., pp. xii, ff.). Owun seldom uses the thorn letter (þ), but in Jn. 18: 1-3, written by Farman, that letter appears seventeen times. The date of the gloss is supposed to belong to the latter half of the tenth century.

B. THE PRINTED EDITIONS.

(Cf. Skeat's Pref. to Mk., pp. xiv, ff.).

I.—The first edition of the West Saxon Gospels was printed by John Day in 1571, at the suggestion of Archbishop Parker. It was probably based on the Bodley MS., with a few corrections from the Cambridge MS.

II.—An edition of the Gothic and the West Saxon Gospels in parallel columns was printed by Junius and Marshall in 1665. The basis of this edition is the preceding edition; but Junius and Marshall made use of the Bodley, Cambridge, Corpus, Hatton and Rushworth MSS.

III.—Mr. Thorpe, in 1842, revised the edition made by Junius and Marshall, though he does not say that his work is not an original edition.

IV.—Dr. Bosworth printed an edition of "The Gothic and Anglo-Saxon Gospels, in parallel columns, with the versions of Wicliffe and Tyndale," in 8vo; London, 1865. It was based on the Corpus MS., and gives the text of that MS. with great exactness.

V.—An edition of the Northumbrian glosses of the Gospels in the Lindisfarne MS. was printed at Gütersloh, in 1857, by Karl Wilhelm Bouterwek. This volume contains an excellent glossary.

VI.—In 1858, the same editor, Herr Bouterwek, printed a volume entitled "Screadunga," which contains, among other things, the Rushworth Latin text and gloss of Mark.

VII.—The Gospels (both the Latin and the Anglo-Saxon)

of the Lindisfarne and Rushworth MSS. were edited for the Surtees Society, in 1854–1865, by Rev. J. Stevenson and Mr. G. Waring.

VIII.—(Cf. Skeat's Pref. to Mk., p. i). Mr. Kemble planned and began an edition of the Gospels in the West Saxon, Northumbrian and Old Mercian versions, synoptically arranged, with collations of all the MSS. Mr. Kemble lived to complete only a little more than the first twenty-four chapters of Matthew. Mr. Hardwick completed the Matthew, and the volume appeared in 1858.

IX.—"The Holy Gospels in Anglo-Saxon, Northumbrian, and Old Mercian versions, synoptically arranged, with collations exhibiting all the readings of all the MSS.; together with the early Latin version as contained in the Lindisfarne MS., collated with the Latin version of the Rushworth MS. Edited for the Syndics of the University Press. by the Rev. Walter W. Skeat, Litt. D., LL.D. Edin., M.A. Oxon., Elrington and Bosworth Professor of Anglo-Saxon, and Fellow of Christ's College, Cambridge. Cambridge : At the University Press, 1871–1887." This is a truly great work, and the benefits that will flow from it to Anglo-Saxon scholarship are incalculable. The more one turns the pages of this great volume, the deeper will grow his respect for its merits, and for the editor, whose patience, fidelity, accuracy, and critical ability can be duly proclaimed only by the volume itself.

X.—In this country, in 1871, the West Saxon Gospel of John with a glossary appeared in a work entitled "Hand-Book of Anglo-Saxon and Early English, by Hiram Corson, M.A." This has been a serviceable pioneer in the advancement of the study of Anglo-Saxon in America, and deserves commendation as such.

XI.—Professor James W. Bright, of the Johns Hopkins University, in 1893, edited from the manuscripts a school edition of the West Saxon Gospel of Luke, with an introduction, notes, and a glossary. The little volume has many merits, one being that it is the forerunner of a "critical edition of the Anglo-Saxon Gospels," to which we shall look forward with interest.

Before proceeding to the consideration of authorship, Professor Skeat's observation regarding the source of the restoration of the last seven verses of Mark in the Royal MS. is worthy of attention. Professor Skeat infers that "the scribe of the Hatton MS. had access to some other MS. besides the Royal." An examination of the text of the restored verses shows that the "other MS." to which the scribe had access could not well have been cognate with any MS. of the Anglo-Saxon Gospels which we possess. But perhaps Professor Skeat means a Latin MS.; for it is possible that the Hatton scribe himself translated the passage from the Latin. Since making this conjecture it has been gratifying to find that Professor Bright entertains the same opinion regarding the possible translation; indeed, he seems to have definitely determined the truth of it; for, in speaking of the *lacunæ* filled by this restoration and others, he states unqualifiedly that the Hatton scribe "supplied them in his own hand and by his own translation from the Latin" (cf. Bright's Luke, p. xvi).

THE AUTHORSHIP OF THE WEST SAXON GOSPELS

The investigation of this subject, it may be well to state at once, was not premeditated, but was prompted by the discovery of certain suggestively distinguishing features of the West Saxon Gospels, which chanced to be noted while the writer was engaged in preparing for publication an edition of the West Saxon Gospel of Mark. The fact that many distinguished scholars and critics had for above three hundred years so thoroughly scrutinized all the Anglo-Saxon Gospels, tended at first to depreciate the significance of certain facts which, nevertheless, ultimately induced this inquiry into the authorship of the West Saxon Gospels. Professor Bright's remark that " There is no clue to the authorship of this version " (cf. Bright's Luke, p. xii), gave zest to the search ; but the warning contained in Professor Skeat's general statement that " Large theories are constantly being built up, like an inverted cone, upon very slender bases " (cf. Skeat's Pref. to Jn., p. xi), chilled the first ardor of enthusiasm.

For the present it has been found impossible to prosecute the investigation in certain desirable lines on account of the lack of trustworthy and time-saving aids beyond a few good texts. Let me not seem, however, to depreciate unduly the zealous labors of great scholars and their valued contributions to the science of Anglo-Saxon philology. There are most estimable works in this department of learning, but the science is still in its infancy, and its critical apparatus must not be judged by the same standards that we are accustomed to apply in testing the merit of contributions to classical philology ; and yet, while we thus excuse the weakness of a science by pleading its tender age, the lack of strength is none the less felt. Let this be illustrated by a particular example. No work is more able to bear up under just criticism than Sievers's Grammar of Old English, so ably translated and edited by our fellow countryman, Professor Albert S. Cook, of Yale University. This work is justly held in the highest esteem by all Anglo-Saxon scholars; and yet, in the present investigation, it has happened to fail at the point where most needed, namely, dialectic forms. In proof of this, one citation will suffice. In Cook's Sievers, paragraph 390, Note 2, it is stated: "Instead of *nóm*, *nómon* LWS. also has *nam*, *námon*." Now, the fact is that (-)*nam*, (-)*namon* is doubly more frequent than (-)*nom*, (-)*nomon* in the very works which in Cook's Sievers (pp. 244, 245) are said to "take precedence of all others . . . among the ancient specimens of West Saxon.". Thus (-)*nam*, (-)*namon* is found in Sw. Alf. C. P., pp. 161: 7; 259: 8; 415: 17; 425: 3; and in Sw. Alf. Oros., pp. 34: 2; 42: 10; 44: 27, 32; 46: 7; 64: 10; 66: 21; 86: 30 (see text); 88: 7; 94: 4, 7; 106: 22; 154: 15; 158: 4; 200: 8; 210: 9; 228: 25; while (-)*nom*, (-)*nomon* occurs in Sw. Alf. C. P., p. 37: 5; and in Sw. Alf. Oros., pp. 42: 29; 50: 7; 148: 18; 166: 27; 218: 30; 230: 28; 252: 10; 280: 26, 27. It is probable that occurrences of each of these forms have been overlooked in making this record, yet the record has been impartially made.

But it has been possible to arrive at certain important conclusions in this inquiry into the authorship of the West Saxon Gospels by the study of good texts alone. These conclusions are (mainly), that the authorship is at least dual, and probably triple; more explicitly, that the Matthew is by one translator, the Mark and Luke by another, and the John by a third (unless possibly by the translator of the Matthew); that the translator of the Matthew and the translator of the John were probably locally akin, possibly translating conjointly; and that the translator of the Mark and Luke was probably distant from the locality where the Matthew and the John were translated, though Dr. Murray has pointed out that inmates of the same monastery may exhibit great linguistic differences by reason of their "different nativity."

Before presenting the evidence on which these conclusions

have been based, attention should be called to the kinds of data to be used or refused in an inquiry like the present. First of all, no great importance should be attached in general to those features of the text that were possibly introduced by scribes. We have seen that the number of scribes engaged in writing a single MS. is mostly determinable by the handwritings; and that in the copies made from this, the evidence of its composite workmanship vanishes. We do not know, for example, whether one or a dozen scribes wrote the MS. from which our oldest MSS. of the West Saxon Gospels are supposed to have been copied. We have seen, furthermore, that scribes often silently copy "restorations" made by their predecessors, and that they themselves often make "restorations" without taking the trouble to notify their readers. We have seen also that in copying a MS., inmates of the same monastery may exhibit very noticeable linguistic differences by reason of their "different nativity." In the case of the Bodley, Royal, and Hatton MSS., which are transcriptions one of another in the order named, we have seen that a scribe may copy a text more or less conformably to the language of his time (cf. Skeat's Pref. to Lk., p. viii). Imagine, then, what linguistic variations a single text may exhibit by reason of coöperative transcription, restorations, conformations, etc.*

Again, in collecting evidence as to authorship, it must be borne in mind that a translator, if a novice, may be expected to exhibit different grades of workmanship; consequently his first efforts should not be cited to prove his last efforts spurious. For example, when the translation of the Lord's Prayer in

---

*The hints thus accidentally given by the MSS. of the Anglo-Saxon Gospels are of manifold importance. They teach especially that those who pass judgment as to the date of a MS. should render a decision only after the most careful and exhaustive investigation. It would be well, too, if the data on which such decisions are based, were fully tabulated for the benefit of all concerned. This is a most vital matter; for when the date of a MS. is supposed to be correctly settled, its dialectal forms, etc., are used in determining the dates of other MSS. Grammars and dictionaries are then founded upon these, and thus not infrequently "a little leaven leaveneth the whole lump."

Matthew is contrasted with that in Luke and is seen to be mechanical, little can be inferred save that, as the translator advances, he frees himself from the improper restraints of the original text.*

We need not be surprised, then, that the translation of the latter half of the Matthew differs in many respects from that of the first half, which is particularly noticeable in the case of transitional particles. We may note also that the Latin *scriba* is translated by *writere* the first two times (Mt. 2: 4; 5: 20); thereafter by *bocere*. The Latin *pharisaei* is translated by *sundorhalgan* until the fifteenth chapter is reached; thereafter in Matthew it is directly transferred, except in Mt. 27: 62. The Latin *crux* in the sense of *burden* is translated by *cwylming* in Mt. 10: 38; Mk. 8: 34; Lk. 9: 23; 14: 27; but by *rod* in Mt. 16: 24, which is probably a mere slip. B. & T. does not note the use of *rod* in this sense.

Again, the use of similar expressions in the translation of parallel passages may often be expected from translators of the Gospels even when the translators are remote from each other in time and place of translation. This is possible chiefly by reason of two things, the simplicity of the thought and the translators' probable previous familiarity in their vernacular with the main stories and memorable sayings of the Gospels, even though that vernacular translation were never committed to writing. The latter fact may be well illustrated by the West Saxon translation of *benedi[c]tus qui uenturus est*, etc. (Mt. 21: 9):

---

*The West Saxon translation of the Lord's Prayer in Matthew begins and ends uniquely—Fæder ure...soðlice. Fæder ure is paralleled in form by Fæder min in Ælfric's half poetical "Lives of Saints" (Sk. Ælf. I, p. 402: 6). As to the ending, it may be said that the use of *Amen* to mark devotional termination occurs throughout the Blickling Homilies and the homilies of Ælfric. (See especially Th. Ælf. I, p. 76: 8, 25). Ælfric has left us a collection of eleven prayers in Anglo-Saxon (Th. Ælf. II, pp. 596, ff.). The first three terminate with *Sy hit swa;* the remaining eight with *Amen.* Surely, *Amen* thus used was as good Anglo-Saxon as it was good Greek or good Latin. The translator of the West Saxon Matthew had, however, possibly as much right to translate the word by soðlice as Ælfric had by *Sy hit swa*.

Sygebletsod sepe com, etc. This faulty translation is doubtless due to the fact that the tense of *venit*, the usual form of the verb in this saying, may have been misunderstood by the Anglo-Saxons; for they seem regularly to have rendered it by *com* (see Mt. 23: 39 (Rush. *cwome*); Mk. 11: 9; Lk. 13: 35; 19: 38; Jn. 12: 13; Th. Ælf. I, pp. 60: 9; 214: 17). But perhaps the best way to show that different translators may often independently make use of the same words and phrases in translating the same passage of the Gospels is to compare passages in the West Saxon version with translations by Alfred, whom no one seems ever to have suspected of being the author of that version. There are numerous examples, but the following best illustrate the point:

Alfred (Sw. C. P., p. 43: 19, 20): Faraðˈ (and) cyðaðˈ minum broðrum ðˈæt hie cumen to Galileum; ðˈær hie me gesceoðˈ.

Cp. MS., Mt. 28: 10: faraðˈ (and) cyþaðˈ minum gebroþrum þ(æt) hig faron on galileam þær hig geseoþ me.

Alfred (Sw. C. P., p. 329: 6, 7): Gewitaðˈ fro(m) me, awiergde, on ece fyr, ðˈæt wæs gegearwod diofle (and) his englum.

Cp. MS., Mt. 25: 41: Gewitaðˈ awyrgyde fram me on þ(æt) éce fyr. þe ys deofle (and) hys englum gegearwud.

Alfred (Sw. C. P., p. 218: 24): On eo[w]rum geðylde ge gehealdaðˈ eowra saula.

Cp. MS., Lk. 21: 19: On eowru(m) geþylde ge gehealdaðˈ eowre sawla.

The work of Alfred's here drawn from had such a wide circulation that it may have affected the diction of our West Saxon version of the Gospels The Blickling Homilies probably exercised little or no effect; and yet the similarity in the language of parallel passages is no less.

Blick. Homl., p. 169: 8-10: Ge næddrena cynn, hwylc æteowde eow to fleonne fram ðon toweardan Godes erre?

Cp. MS., Mt. 3: 7: La næddrena cyn. hwa geswutelode eow to fleonne fra(m) þan toweardan yrre: progenies uiperarum quis demonstrauit uobis fugere á futura ira?

Cp. MS., Lk. 3: 7: eala næddrena cynn hwa æt-ywde eow þ(æt) ge fleon fra(m) þam towerdan yrre: genimina uiperaru(m) quis ostendit uobis fugire a uentura ira?

From these comparisons it will be manifest that likeness in the translations of an ordinary passage of the Gospels does not necessarily indicate a common translator.

On the other hand, a single translator may make different renderings of the same passage. Ælfric well illustrates this:

Grein's Ælf., Gen. 3: 5: Ac god vât sôðlîce, þät eóvre eágan beóð geopenode on svâ hvılcum däge, svâ ge etaðof þam treove, and ge beóð þonne englum gelîce vitende ægðer ge gôd ge yfel.

Th. Ælf. I, p. 18: 2, ff.: ac God wát genoh gearc, gif ge of ðam treowe geetað, þonne beoð eowere eagan geopenode, and ge magon geseon and tocnáwan ægðer ge gód ge yfel, and ge beoð englum gelice.

From all these considerations, it will be apparent that evidence as to authorship should be mainly founded, not upon features of the text that may be due to the nativity or caprice of scribes, to restorations and conformations, to the simplicity of the thought, or to the influence of previous translations; but upon characteristics,—characteristics which are deep-seated, and which run through the whole body of the text or the major portion of it. Most of the data presented as evidence in this paper will be seen individually to fulfill these requirements; while, on the other hand, a few of the data must be taken conjointly in order to embrace the whole text and be of much significance.

THE EVIDENCE OF COMPOSITE AUTHORSHIP.

Although it is unnecessary to go beyond the text of the West Saxon version of the Gospels to prove indisputably its composite authorship, yet it has seemed advisable to cite for comparison works whose authorship is unquestionably single. Accordingly, where it has been found practicable and worth the labor involved, comparison of the Gospels in certain respects has been made with Alfred's Orosius and Cura Pastoralis, with the Blickling Homilies, with Ælfric's Homilies, and the first half of his Lives of Saints, and with the portion of Ælfric's works edited by Grein. The testimony of the Northumbrian and Old

Mercian Gospels is sometimes to the point; and the fragments of the Gothic Gospels have been thought worthy of citation in one or two instances. It should be remarked that Morris's glossary to the Blickling Homilies though probably accurate is incomplete. For example, the occurrence of *heofenum* on p. 125: 29, and of *heofenas* on p. 139: 2, we do not find recorded in the glossary. Statements in this paper as to the non-occurrence of words in the Blickling Homilies are based upon personal reading, and not upon that glossary. The glossary, however, has been used as a check.

We shall now present the data of evidence as to the composite authorship of the West Saxon version of the Gospels, not in the order of discovery, but in the order which for various reasons seems best suited to the case. Peculiarities regarding the word *heofon*, however, were among the first to attract attention, and will be the first presented.

i. HEOFON, HEOFONE.

This word has proved doubly useful in the present inquiry. It has been found peculiar in one respect in Matthew, and in another respect in John, thus dividing the Gospels into three distinct groups: Matthew—Mark and Luke—John. The peculiarity in Matthew is the occurrence of both the weak and the strong forms. There are 18 instances of the weak forms of *heofon* scattered throughout this Gospel, while neither in Mark and Luke nor in John is a single occurrence of a weak form to be found.*

If we turn to the Orosius and the Cura Pastoralis, we find no weak form of *heofon*. The word itself, however, is in these works infrequently met with. In the Blickling Homilies the strong forms are of very frequent occurrence, while no instance of a weak form is to be noted. Ælfric uses both the strong and the weak forms side by side, and everywhere so frequently that citations need not be made.

---

*It should be observed that *seo heofon* occurs in Lk. 4: 25; but "In L W S. *séo* is used for *se*" (Cook's Sievers, par. 337, Note 2). In the Blickling Homilies, *seo heofon* and *se heofon* occur on the same page (p. 93: 4, 22).

John is separated from the other Gospels by the fact that in this Gospel *heofon* is at variance with the Latin original as to number, 15 out of 19 times. In the other Gospels great care was apparently taken to have the number of *heofon* in agreement with the number of *caelum;* and only 11 out of 133 occurrences show disagreement. In the following list of the occurrences of *heofon* or *caelum*, *w* denotes *weak;* *sp* or *ps* means singular for plural or *vice versa;* and [ ] or ( ) means that the word *caelum* or *heofon* is wanting:

Singular

Matthew	Mark and Luke	John
5: 18, 34	4: 32	3: 31
6: 20W, 26W	6: 41	6: 31, 33
8: 20W	7: 34	12: 28
11: 23, 25	8: 11	
13: 32W	11: 30, 31	
14: 19	13: 25, 27	
16: 1, 2, (3), 3	13: 31, 32	
21: 25	14: 62	
22: 30	2: 15	
23: 22W	3: 21, 22	
24: 29W, 29 sp, W	4: 25	
24: 30W, 30W, 35W	8: 5	
26: 64	9: 16, 54, 58	
28: 2W, 18W	10: 15, 18, 21	
	11: [2], [2]	
	11: 13, 16	
	13: 19	
	15: 7, 21	
	16: 17	
	17: 21, 24, 29	
	18: 13, 22	
	20: 4, 5	
	21: 11, 26sp	
	21: 33	
	22: 43	
	24: 51	
	6: [35]	
	12: 56	

Plural

Matthew	Mark and Luke	John
3: 2, 16, 17	1: 10, 11, [15]	1: 32ps, 51ps
4: 17	10: [14], 21ps	3: 13ps, 13ps
5: 3, 10W, 12	11: 25, (26)	3: 13ps, 27ps
5: 16, 19W, 19W	12: 25	6: 32ps, 32ps
5: 20W, 45	13: 25	6: 38ps, 41ps
6: 1, 9, 10ps	16: 19ps	6: 42ps, 50ps
7: 11, 21, 21, 21	4: [30]	6: 51ps, 58ps
8: 11	6: 23ps	17: 1ps
10: 7, 32, 33	10: 20	
11: 11, 12	12: 33	
12: 50W	15: 18ps	
13: 11, 24, 31, 33, 44	19: 38ps	
13: 45, 47, 52W		
16: 17, 19, 19, 19		
18: 1, 3, 4, (10), (10)		
18: 14, 18ps, 18ps, 19, 23		
19: 12, 14, 21, (23), 24		
20: 1; 21: 25ps		
22: 2; 23: 9, 13		
24: 31, (36)		
25: 1		

These irregularities might be lamely explained by supposing interruptions and long delays in the work of translating; but as new data are introduced, this supposition will be seen to be wholly worthless. Moreover, in this particular case, it may be said that the weak form of *heofon* should be least expected to be found in Matthew, which we have seen to be the work of a novice in Gospel translation; for, from what we are able to ascertain at present, we judge that the weak form of *heofon* is late, and therefore to be looked for in an author's later rather than in his earlier compositions if to be looked for only in one of these divisions. As to the discrepancies in number between *heofon* in the translation and *cælum* in the original, it is difficult to imagine how a translator could be so exact 122 out of 133 opportunities and then negligent 15 out of 19 times. Moreover, it will be observed that in John the plural is used for the singular 15 out of 19 times (the Latin being always singular in John). This might be explained by supposing that the translator had become accustomed to writing the plural in Luke; but in Luke *heofon* is put in the plural only 5 times, while it is in the singular 33 times.

ii. UNDERFON, ONFON.

The occurrences of these synonymous words divide the Gospels again into the three groups—Matthew—Mark and Luke—John. Matthew has both words, but *onfon* occurs the more frequently; Mark and Luke have only *onfon;* and John again has both words, but *underfon* occurs 22 times while *onfon* is found only three times.

Here, again, we find our known authors uniform respecting the employment of *underfon* and *onfon*. In the Blickling Homilies *underfon* is not to be found, while the occurrence of *onfon* is very frequent (Morris records 65 occurrences). Ælfric uses *underfon* almost to the exclusion of *onfon*. A moderately careful record, based upon personal reading, shows that *onfon* occurs 30 times in Ælfric's Homilies, 7 times in vol. I of his Lives of Saints, and 5 times in the volume by Grein. Alfred uses *underfon* and *onfon* interchangeably, and with about equal frequency.

The following citations from the Cura Pastoralis will show that Alfred regarded the words as synonymous:

underfon

p. 75: 20 *suscipio*	p. 267:13 *percipio*
105: 24 "	288: 5 "
193: 6 *accipio*	293: 3 *suscipio*
197: 25 *concipio*	301: 25 *decipio*
253: 4 *recipio*	335: 14 *accipio*
255: 12 "	367: 10, 11, 17 *concipio*
263: 21 *accipio*	369: 7 *accipio*
267: 3 "	409: 18, 22 *capio*

onfon

p. 81: 19 *accipio*	p. 293: 25 *recipio*
85: 21 *recipio*	345: 21 *percipio*
91: 20 *suscipio*	371: 21 *accipio*
97: 2 *concipio*	377: 12 *percipio*
121: 10 *suscipio*	381: 5 *recipio*
139: 9 "	391: 15, 15 "
145: 18 *accipio*	399: 30 *suscipio*
203: 12 *suscipio*	429: 12 *percipio*

In the West Saxon Gospels the record is strangely as follows:

MATTHEW

underfon

10: 14   *recipio*
10: 40, 40   "
10: 40, 40   "
10: 41, 41   "
19: 11   *capio*
25: 16, 17, 18 *accipio*
25: 20, 22, 24   "
27: 27   *suscipio*

MARK AND LUKE

underfon

(not found)

JOHN

underfon

1: 11, 12 *recipio*
3: 11, 27 *accipio*
3: 32, 33   "
4: 45   *excipio*
5: 41, 43 *accipio*
5: 43, 44   "
7: 39   "
12: 48   "
13: 20, 20   "
13: 20, 20   "
14: 17   "
16: 24   "
17: 8   "
18: 3   "
20: 22   "

MATTHEW

onfon

1: 20, 24   *accipio*
2: 21   "
6: 2, 5, 16   *recipio*
7: 8   *accipio*
8: 17   "
10: 8, 41, 41   "
13: 20, 33   "
18: 5, 5   *suscipio*
19: 29   *accipio*
20: 9, 10, 10   "
21: 34   "
25: 34   *possideo*
26: 26   *accipio*
27: 6, 9   "
28: 15   "

MARK AND LUKE

onfon

4: 16   *accipio*
4: 20   *suscipio*
4: 36   *adsumo*
6: 41   *accipio*
9: 37, 37 *recipio*
9: 37, 37 *suscipio*
10: 15   *recipio*
10: 30   *accipio*
11: 24   "
12: 2, 40   "
14: 23   "
15: 23   "

onfon

2: 26, 28   *accipio*
6: 34   "
6: 34   *recipio*
8: 13   *suscipio*
8: 40   *excipio*
9: 5   *recipio*
9: 11   *excipio*
9: 48   *suscipio*
9: 48, 48   *recipio*
9: 48, 53   "
10: 8   *suscipio*
10: 10   *recipio*
10: 38   *excipio*
11: 10   *accipio*
13: 19, 21   "
15: 2, 27   *recipio*
16: 4, 9   "
16: 25, 25 (sc.) "
18: 17   *accipio*
18: 30   *recipio*
19: 6   *excipio*
19: 12, 15   *accipio*
19: 23   *exigo*
20: 47   *accipio*
22: 17, 17, 19   "
23: 41   *recipio*
24: 30   *accipio*

JOHN

onfon

1: 16 *accipio*
5: 34   "
19: 30   "

Comment can add but little force to the testimony of the words *heofon, onfon* and *underfon*. Especially does the almost exclusive use of *underfon* in John separate that Gospel not only from Mark and Luke, but also from Matthew. The entire absence of *underfon* in Mark and Luke gives moral certainty that they are not by the translator of John. It is perhaps more remarkable than noteworthy that the beginning and end (which Professor Skeat has quoted) of the homily inserted between Mark and Luke in the Corpus MS. reveal the alien character of the homily by the use of the weak form of *heofon* and by the use of *underfon* twice: M(en) þa l(eofestan). Her onginð þ(æt) halie g(e)writ þe co(m) fra(m) heofenan into hierusale(m) ... and se þe underfehð witigan on þæs witigan naman he underfehð þæs witigan mede (cf. Skeat's Pref. to Mk., p. v). *

* The Rushworth Gospels do not contain *underfon;* but the Lindisfarne Jn. 4: 45 has *underfengon* added after *genomun* in glossing *exceperunt.*

iii. þÆT HE WOLDE, ETC.

In direct confirmation of the testimony of *heofon, underfon* and *onfon*, is the use of *willan* (occasional in Matthew, wanting in Mark and Luke, but frequent in John) after the final conjunction þ æ t in translating Latin infinitives of purpose, and subjunctives after final *ut*, when the leading verb is in an historical tense. There is probably not a sample of this use of *willan* in the works of Alfred and Ælfric which are quoted in this paper; though final clauses depending on a past tense are especially frequent in the Orosius. *Magan,* *motan and sculan, however, are at times introduced into such clauses, while *sculan* and *willan* are freely used to translate the Latin future.

In the quotations given below, the passages from Jn. 4: 7, 8 are introduced, though they are not exact specimens of the point in illustration; but they are unparalleled in the other Gospels and show the translator's perplexity in trying to bring out most clearly the full meaning of the Latin final infinitive.

Mt. 22: 11: ϸa eode se cyning in þ(æt) he *wolde* geseon: intrauit autem rex ut uideret.

Mt. 28: 1: com seo magdalenisce maria (and) seo oðer maria þ(æt) hig *woldon* geseon þa byrgene: uenit maria magdalenæ et altera maria uidere sepulchrum.

Mk. 16: 1: [hi] bohton wyrt-gemang þ(æt) hi comon (and) hine smyredon: emerunt aromata ut unientes ungerent eum.

Jn. 4: 7: þa com þær an wif of samária *wolde* wæter feccan: uenit mulier de samaria haurire aquam.

Jn. 4: 8: His leorning-cnihtas ferdon þa to þære ceastre *woldon* hi(m) mete bicgan: discipuli enim eius abierant in ciuitate(m) ut cibos emerent.

Jn. 11: 19: Manega ... comon ... þ(æt) hig *woldon* hi frefrian: multi ... uenerant ... ut consolarentur eas.

Jn. 11: 55: manega foron ... þ(æt) hig *woldon* hig sylfe gehalgian: ascenderunt multi ... ut sanctificarent sé ipsos.

Jn. 12: 9: hig comon ... þ(æt) hig *woldon* geseon ladzaru(m): uenerunt ... ut lazarum uiderent.

Jn. 12: 20: þe foron þ(æt) hig *woldon* hi gebiddan: qui ascenderant ut adorarent.

Blick. Homl., p. 33: 12, 13: Nis þ(æt) to wundrigenne þeah þe he wære costod, se to þon cóm þ(æt) hé acweald beon *wolde*.

Mt. 22: 15: Da ongunnon þa pharisei rædan þ(æt) hig *woldon* þone hælend on hys spræce befon: Tunc abeuntes pharisaei consilium inierunt ut caperent eum in sermone.

Mt. 26: 4: (and) hig hæfdon mycel ge-mot þ(æt) hig *woldon* þone hælend mid (MS. mit) facne besyrwan (and) ofslean : et consilium fecerunt ut i(esu)m dolo tenerent et occiderent.

Mk. 14: 1: þa sohton þa heah-sacerdas (and) þa boceras hu hi hine mid facne namon (and) of-slogon: Et quaerebant summi sacerdotes et scribae quomodo eum dolo tenerent et occiderent.

Lk. 22: 2: (and) þara sacerda ealdras (and) þa boceras smeadon hu hig hine forspildon: Et quaerebant principes sacerdotu(m) et scribae quomodo eum interficerent.

Mt. 26: 16: he smeade geornlice þ(æt) he hyne *wolde* belæwan: quaerebat oportunitatem ut eum traderet.

Mt. 27: 7: Hig worhton þa gemót (and) smeadon hu hig *sceoldon* þæs hælendes wurð ateon: consilio autem inito.

Mk. 3: 6: þa pharisei . . . þeahtedon ongen hine. hu hi hine fordon *mihton*: pharisaei . . . consilium faciebant aduersus eum quomodo eum perderent.

Lk. 19: 47: [hi] smeadon hu hig hine fordon *mihton**: quaerebant illum perdere.

Mk. 14: 11: he smeade he hu hine digellice sealde: querebat quomodo illum oportune traderet.

Lk. 22: 6: he sohte hu he eaȝelicust hine . . . gesealde: quaerebat oportunitatem ut traderet illum.

Jn. 10: 39: Hig smeadon witodlice embe þ(æt) hig *woldon* hine gefon: Quaerebant ergo eum perdere.

Jn. 11: 8: nu þa iudeas sohton ðe þ(æt) hig *woldon* þe hænan: nunc quærebant té lapidare iudaei.

Jn. 11: 53: hig þohton þ(æt) hi *woldon* hyne ofslean: cogitauerunt ut interficerent eum.

Jn. 12: 10: [hi] þohton þ(æt) hig *woldon* lazaru(m) ofslean: cogitauerunt . . . ut et lazarum interficerent.

Blick. Homl., p. 77: 7, 8: Þa ealdormen þara sacerda þohtan þ(æt) hie *woldan* Lazarum ofsléan.

Jn. 7: 32: Ða ealdras (and) ða pharisei sendon hyra þenas þ(æt) hig *woldon* hine gefón: Et miserunt principes et pharisaei ministros ut appraehenderunt eum.

Mk. 12: 13: þa sendon hi to hi(m) sume . . . þ(æt) hi befengon hine on his worde: Et mittunt ad eum quosdam . . . ut eum caperent in uerbo.

Lk. 20: 20: Ða sendun hig mid searwu(m) þa ðe riht-wise léton þ(æt) hig hine gescyldgudun (and) þ(æt) hig hine gesealdon: Et obseruantes miserunt insidiatores qui sé iustos simularent ut caperent eum in sermone et traderent eum.

Jn. 8: 59: hig namon stánas to þa(m) þ(æt) hig *woldon* hyne torfian: tulerunt ergo lapides ut iacerent in eum.

Jn. 10: 31: Ða iudeas namon stanas þ(æt) hig *woldon* hyne torfian: sustulerunt lapides iudaei ut lapidarent eum.

---

*Note the common phraseology of Mark and Luke.

Jn. 11: 51, 52: he witgode þ(æt) se hælend sceolde sweltan . . . þ(æt) he *wolde* gesomnian togædere godes bearn: prophetauit quia i(esu)s moriturus erat . . . ut filios d(e)i . . . congregaret in unum.

The following quotations are remotely akin to the preceding and are given for the sake of completeness:

Mt. 25: 10: Witodlice þa hig ferdun (and) *woldon* bycgean: dum autem irent emere. (See Jn. 4: 7, 8, cited above; also Jn. 14: 2).

Mt. 27: 15: Hig hæfdon heo(m) to ge-wunan to heora symbel-dæge þ(æt) se dema *sceolde* forgyfan þa(m) folce ænne forwyrhtne mann: Per diem autem sollemnem consueuerat praeses dimittere populo unum uinctum.

Mk. 15: 6: On symmel-dæge wæs his gewuna þ(æt) he hi(m) for-geafe ænne gebundenne: Per diem autem festum dimittere solebat illis unum ex uinctis.

Jn. 4: 4: hi(m) g(e)byrode þ(æt) he *sceolde* faran: Oportebat autem eum transire.

Jn. 5: 27: he . . . sealde hi(m) anweald þ(æt) he *moste* deman: potestatem dedit ei et iudicium facere.

Jn. 7: 1: þa iudéas hine sohton (and) *woldon* hyne ofsléan: quaerebant eu(m) iudaei interficere.

Jn. 9:39: Ic com on þysne middan-eard to demenne þ(æt) þa *sceolon* geseon, þe ne g(e)seoð: in iudicium ego in hunc mundum ueni ut qui non uident uideant.

Jn. 11: 57; þa bisceopas (and) þa pharisei hæfdon beboden gif hwa wiste hwar he wære þ(æt) he hyt cydde þ(æt) hig *mihton* hine niman: dederant autem pontifices et pharisaei mandatum ut si quis cognouerit ubi sit indicet ut apprachendant eum.

Jn. 12: 5: Hwi ne sealde heo þas sealfe: . . . þ(æt) man *mihte* syllan þearfon: quare hoc ungentum non uenit . . . et datum est egenis? (See Mt. 26: 8, 9; Mk. 14: 4, 5).

Jn. 19: 38: iosep . . . bæd pilatus þ(æt) He *moste* niman þæs hælendes lichaman: rogauit pilatum ioseph . . . ut tolleret corpus i(es)u.

Jn. 20: 9: hit gebyrede þ(æt) he sceolde fram deaðe arisan: oporteret eum á mortuis resurgere.*

To appreciate fully this remarkable usage of *willan*, the reader should not only consider carefully the preceding quotations, but also read through Mark or Luke and then John. The method of expressing past purpose in John is so strongly contrasted with the method in Mark and Luke, that it seems impossible for anyone to read these Gospels consecutively or otherwise and fail to observe the contrast.

iv. þÆRA, þARA, ETC.

Variation in the use of the forms þæra, þara, þær, þar, hwær, hwar may be due to scribal caprice and indicate merely that some ancestral MS. was executed by several scribes; but the variation is uniform in the Corpus, Bodley, and Cotton MSS., tallying exactly with what we have already found separating the Gospels into the groups—Matthew—Mark and Luke—John—and is, therefore, probably to be considered a dialectic variation, pointing to composite authorship.

---

*If any one desires to examine all the cases where *magan, *motan, *sculan*, or *willan* is introduced into the West Saxon text without authority from the Latin original, let him consult the following references, in addition to what has been above quoted:

Mt. 8: 25; 11: 3; 12: 26; 13: 28; 16: 25; 18: 21; 20: 10; 24: 42, 43, 43, 44; 26: 5, 54, 60; 27: 49.

Mk. 4: 13; 6: 23; 10: 15.

Lk. 7: 19, 20; 8: 27; 9: 53; 10: 24; 12: 39; 14: 19, 31, 32; 19: 4; 21: 14, 21; 23: 14; 24: 28.

Jn. 4: 35; 6: 6, 15, 21, 64; 7: 35, 35, 39; 8: 5; 10: 32; 11: 8, 11; 12: 19, 33; 13: 1, 6, 11, 27; 14: 2, 22; 15: 4, 20; 17: 20; 19: 15; 21: 3, 3, 19, 21, 25.

Mk. 10: 15; Lk. 21: 14, 21; 24: 28; etc., perhaps do not properly belong to this list.

32 THE AUTHORSHIP OF

MATTHEW	MARK AND LUKE		JOHN	
Gen. pl. of *se*	Gen. pl. of *se*	Gen. pl. of *se*	Gen. pl. of *se*	
þ æ r a	þ a r a	þ a r a	þ a r a	þ æ r e
2: 4	1: 44	1: 1, 4, 71	2: 15	6: 45
3: 7, 7, 10	2: 26	3: 2	3: 15, 20	þ æ r a
5: 20, 28	6: 43, 44	4: 26	4: 13, 14	7: 13, 48, 48
7: 8, 21, 24, 26	7: 27, 28	5: 9	6: 71	þ æ r e
10: 2	12: 23, 43	6: 47	11: 19, 26, 45	10: 32
13: 19, 49	þ æ r a	10: 36	12: 9, 10, 46	þ æ r a
14: 20, 21	11: 18	11: 4, 10	13: 28	12: 2, 42
16: 3, 9, 10, 14, 21		13: 1	15: 2	13: 23
20: 18		14: 24	20: 23	18: 9, 12, 22, 37
21: 8 45		19: 47.		19: 12, 20, 42
22: 28		20: 1, 19, 39		þ æ r e
23: 30, 31		22: 2, 4, 50, 66		19: 34, 38
24: 8, 29		23: 10, 13		þ æ r a
25: 19, 29				20: 19, 19, 23, 25
26: 3, 3, 14, 47		þ æ r a		þ æ r e
26: 51, 51, 56		22: 54		20: 25
26: 57, 58, 59, 60				þ æ r a
26: 62, 63, 65				21: 2, 6, 11, 12
27: 1, 3, 6, 12				
27: 20, 41, 62				
28: 11				
þ a r a				
21: 12, 12, 15				
21: 23, 31, 34				

MATTHEW	MARK AND LUKE		JOHN	
Adverb	Adverb	Adverb	Adverb	
þ æ r	þ a r	þ a r	þ a r	þ æ r
2: 9, 13, 15	1: 35, 38	2: 6	2: 12	1: 24, 28
3: 16	2: 4, 6	4: 16, 17, 31	3: 8	2: 1
4: 20	3: 1, 31	5: 12, 29	5: 10	3: 22, 23
5: 23, 24, 37	4: 5, 15	6: 12	6: 3, 12, 23, 24	4: 6, 7, 27, 40, 46
6: 19, 19, 20, 21, 21 33	5: 11, 14, 40	7: 12, 12, 49	7: 34, 36, 42, 42	þ æ r a
7: 25, 25, 27	6: 5, 10, 46, 53, 55	8: 32, 33, 35, 56	8: 9	4: 40
8: 12, 26, 30, 32	8: 9	9: 4, 14, 17	9: 13	þ æ r
10: 11, 20	9: 44, 46, 48	10: 6, 6	10: 40	5: 5, 6, 13
12: 10, 45, 46	11: 2, 5, 13, 13	11: 26	þ a r a	6: 10, 22, 62
13: 2, 5, 42, 50, 58	13: 14	12: 34, 34	11: 15, 31	8: 9
14: 23, 23	14: 3, 47, 69	13: 1, 11, 22, 28	þ a r	11: 54, 56
15: 29, 38	þ a r a	14: 2	11: 30, 32, 38, 39	12: 2, 9, 26, 26, 29
18: 20, 20	14: 15	15: 13	12: 1	14: 3
19: 2	þ a r	17: 23	13: 30	18: 1, 16
20: 10	15: 35. 39, 46	19: 2	17: 24	19: 18, 19, 20
21: 33	16: 7	21: 21	18: 20, 22	20: 12, 19
22: 11, 11, 13	þ æ r	22: 11, 55	19: 34, 41, 41, 42	21: 9, 18
24: 23, 51	13: 21	þ a r a	20: 11	
25: 24, 24, 26, 26, 30	16: 6	22: 12	21: 8, 12	
26: 7, 57, 71, 73		þ a r		
27: 35, 47, 48		23: 33, 47		
27: 51, 54, 55, 61		24: 12, 14		
28: 2, 2, 7, 10, 11, 16, 17		þ æ r		
þ a r		13: 25		
6: 20		18: 37		
21: 9, 9, 17		22: 49		

Matthew	Mark and Luke		John	
Adverb	Adverb	Adverb	Adverb	Adverb
h w æ r	h w a r	h w a r	h w a r	h w æ r
2: 2, 4	6: 56	8: 25	1: 38, 39	6: 5
8: 20	14: 9, 14, 14	9: 6, 58	7: 11	8: 10
24: 28	15: 47	17: 37, 37	8: 19	
26: 13, 17	16: 20	22: 9, 11	9: 12	
h w a r	h w æ r	h w æ r	11: 34, 57	
15: 33	9: 18	17: 17	20: 2, 13, 14, 15	

Under the supposition that the authorship of these Gospels is composite, the seemingly inexplicable irregularity in the use of the forms þæra, þara, etc., becomes a perfect harmony and a convincing testimony, disturbed only by the six occurrences of þara as a gen. pl. and the two occurrences of the adverbial form þar in Mt. 21, which ought perhaps to be regarded as indicating merely the presence of a "different and conforming hand" in an ancestral MS.

The five distributed occurrences of þære as a gen. pl. in John are full of significance. They especially point out the probable accuracy of the Corpus scribe in comparison with the scribes of the Bodley, Cotton, and Cambridge MSS. The readings of these MSS. are:

Corpus MS.

Jn. 6: 45 ðære; Bodley, Cambridge, þæra; Cotton, ðæra.
    10: 32 þære; Bodley, Cotton, þære; Cambridge, þæra.
    19: 34 þære; Bodley, Cambridge, þæra; Cotton, ——.
    19: 38 þære; Bodley, þære; Cambridge, þæra; Cotton, ——.
    20: 25 ðære; Bodley, ——; Cambridge, ðære; Cotton, þæra.

The appearance of the rare adverbial form þara in Mk. 14: 15 and Lk. 22: 12 is noteworthy. The form is possibly more emphatic than þar. Professor Bright in his edition of Luke has substituted þar for þara in Lk. 22: 12. The passage is parallel with the passage in Mark containing þara as an adverb. All the MSS. have þara in both passages, excepting that the Hatton MS. has þare in Mk. 14: 15. Elsewhere in Mark and Luke the form used is þar. In view of all these facts, ought not the employment of þara instead of þar in these two parallel passages to be regarded as intentional? To whatever cause these two occurrences may be due, they link the two texts at these two points inseparably together.*

V. WITODLICE.

The Northumbrian and Old Mercian Gospels, the West Saxon Matthew and John, and Ælfric's translations from the Old Testament, consulted in any portion, will show that witodlice and soðlice had little if any difference in meaning in the minds of the translators. In the West Saxon Mark and Luke, however, a distinction seems evidently to have been made.

All the occurrences of witodlice and soðlice in the West Saxon Gospels have been carefully collected, and the Latin original has in each case been noted for use in this investigation; but the records are too bulky to be printed in full. The point most deserving of attention is the use of witodlice interchangeably with soðlice as a translation of *autem*. This is frequent in Matthew and John, but occurs only once in Mark and once in Luke.

MATTHEW *Witodlice* =*autem*	MARK *Witodlice* =*autem*	LUKE *Witodlice* =autem	JOHN *Witodlice* =*autem*
1: 21	13: 31	5: 15	3: 21
3: 4			4: 39
8: 10, 12, 33			8: 35, 45, 50
9: 16			11: 1
14: 24			16: 7
15: 38			17: 20, 25
16: 3, 13			18: 2, 14, 18, 36, 40
19: 23			19: 9, 19, 38, 41
21: 8, 13, 15, 32, 38			20: 1, 4, 11, 24, 31
22: 14, 25			21: 4, 18, 19, 25
23: 12			
24: 13, 37			
25: 6, 10, 18, 31			
26: 5, 26, 29, 32, 59			
27: 1, 39, 45, 54, 55, 62			
28: 4, 17			

It should be remarked that the usage in Matthew respecting witodlice and soðlice as equivalents of *autem* is ex-

---

*Here we would call attention to the possible advantage of permitting a well-supported text to remain unchanged. There is no telling what use a bright-eyed pupil may some day make of an unusual reading. Hence it is best to let an odd reading remain in the text where it will be likely to be observed.

tremely variable. In the first half of that Gospel the use of
s o x l i c e is excessive, particularly from the fifth to the thirteenth chapter inclusive. The irregularity, as we have before
intimated, probably indicates only the natural change in the
translator as he becomes familiar with his task.

vi. H A N A, C O C C.

If the history of these words on English soil could be ascertained, it would probably be found to reveal a long contest between them whereby *hana* was ultimately driven from the realm.
The scanty traces of the history that we do possess indicate
that *hana* did not surrender all the territory at once, and
probably the two contestants occupied some localities for a
time in common. The Gothic Gospels, the Northumbrian
Gospels and the Old Mercian Matthew have *hana* only. In
Sweet's glossary to his "Oldest English Texts" (p. 465), *-hana*
in composition is cited 8 times; while *cocc* is not cited at all.
Ælfric uses *hana* in relating Peter's denial (Th. Ælf. II, pp. 246:
4; 248: 33). Alfred has *cocc* in two passages of serious discourse
(Sw. Alf. C. P., pp. 459: 29, 31, 32; 461: 1, 12). When we turn
to the West Saxon Gospels, we find the two words grouping the
Gospels just as, at this stage of our inquiry, might be expected:

MATTHEW		MARK AND	LUKE	JOHN
26: 34	*cocc*	14: 30, 68 *hana*	22: 34 *hána*	13: 38 *cocc*
26: 74, 75	"	14: 72, 72 "	22: 60, 61 "	18: 27 "

This remarkable variation in the translation of the Latin
gallus presumably indicates that the time or place of the translation of the Matthew and the John was not the same as that of
the Mark and Luke.*

Professor Skeat has noted that the Hatton MS. has *coc* for
hana in Lk. 22: 60. The fact, however, is that the Hatton MS.
does not use *hana* at all, thus indicating that *hana* had become
obsolete, or had never existed, in the scribe's vocabulary.

---

*The occurrence of *hancred* in Mt. 14: 25 doubtless indicates a survival in
composition of an obsolete or obsolescent word, just as does our use *of poll-tax,
poll-evil, spider-wort,* etc.

vii. STRIDOR DENTIUM.

This phrase occurs six times in the Latin of Matthew and once in Luke. As usual, the translation in Luke differs from that in Matthew:

Matthew		Luke
8: 12	toþa gristbitung.	13: 28 toþa gryst-lung.
13: 42, 50	" "	
22: 13	" "	
24: 51	" "	
25: 30	" "	

viii. FULGOR.

The translation of this word is worthy of attention,—as the word used in Luke (*lig-ræsc*) is not the usual West Saxon term for lightning. In Matthew *ligyt* is used, and it is employed exclusively by Ælfric in the works cited in this paper (Th. Ælf. I, pp. 222: 31, 32; 504: 30; II, pp. 184: 5; 196: 24; 202: 22, 27; Sk. Ælf. I, p. 114: 22; Grein's Ælf., Ex. 9: 23; 19: 16; Deut. 32: 41; Job, p. 265: 1).

Matthew	Luke
24: 27 *ligyt*	10: 18 *lig-ræsc*
28: 3 "	11: 36 "
	17: 24 "

ix. CENTURIO.

The rendering of this word separates Matthew from Mark and Luke.

Matthew.	Mark and Luke.
8: 5, 8, 13 *hundredes ealdor*	15: 39, 44 *hundred-man* 7: 2, 6 *hundred-man*
27: 54 (*Centori*) " "	23: 47 "

Hundredes ealdor occurs in Th. Ælf. I, pp. 126: 5, 8, 21, 23; 128: 19, 20, 30; 132: 31; 134: 1; II, pp. 258: 7, 33; 418: 33; Sk. Ælf. I, p. 226: 26; 484: 34; 486: 1. In three particular instances, however, (Grein's Ælf., Ex. 18: 21, 25; Deut. 1: 15), *hundredman* is used instead of *hundredes ealdor*, doubtless on account of the influence of other words in the context (see passages cited). This slight irregularity in Ælfric's usage does not explain the case in the Gospels. The passages in Matthew are widely separated, and so likewise are those in Luke. The repetition in Mt. 27: 54 of *hundredes ealdor* from the eighth chapter would lead us to expect the same phrase in Mark and Luke if the translator were the same.

X. VOX CLAMANTIS.

This phrase seems to have troubled translators. The best MSS. of Ælfric have *Clypiende stemn* (Sk. Ælf. I, p. 332: 27). A scribe might easily corrupt the true rendering *clypiendes stemn* into *clypiende stemn*. The corpus scribe Ælfric, however, favored the present inquiry and confirmed his good reputation for accuracy when he wrote:

MATTHEW	MARK	AND	LUKE	JOHN
3: 3 *Clypiendes stefn*	1: 3 *clypiende stefn*		3: 4 *Clypiende stéfen*	1: 23 *clypiendes stéfn*

xi. UPPAN (ON-UPPAN).

The use of *uppan* in Mt. 24: 2, 3, for which Mark and Luke in the parallel passages (Mk. 13: 2, 3 ; Lk. 19: 44; 21: 6) have *ofer* or *on*, confirmed my conviction that the subject of the authorship of these Gospels was worthy of an investigation. Search revealed the significant fact that Matthew has *uppan* (*on-uppan*) 15 times and John 6 times, where Mark and Luke, if represented, regularly have *ofer* or *on* (once *on-ufan*). In these cases the original force of *upp-* is lost; and the compound expresses simply super-position Hence þa astigon hig uppan þæne hróf (Lk. 5: 19) and he . . . stah up on án treow (Lk. 19: 4) cannot be cited as parallels to the citations from Matthew and John. The word (*a*)*stigan* is very frequently accompanied with a distinguishing adverb to define the direction: ne stihð he nyðer (Lk. 17: 31). Furthermore, (*a*)*stigan up*(*p*) is very frequent, and often followed by *to* (see Th. Ælf. I, pp. 22: 20; 182: 29; II, pp. 16: 31; 196: 32; 384: 32; 596: 14, etc., etc.). Yet the *up*(*p*) and the *to* are always written separately, as should be the *up*(*p*) and the *an* (*on*) when the *up*(*p*) has its original force, as in the cases just cited from Luke.

While the reader is examining the following quotations, he would do well to consult the Northumbrian and Old Mercian

Gospels, which are in remarkable harmony with the West Saxon of Mark and Luke :

Mt. 5: 14: seo ceaster . . . þe byð *uppan* múnt aset: ciuitas . . . supra monte posita.

Mt. 9: 18: sete þine hand *uppan* hig: impone manu(m) super eam.

Mt. 10: 27: þ(æt) ge on eare gehyrað bodiaþ *uppan* hrofu(m): quod in aure auditis praedicate sup(er) tecta

Lk. 12: 3: þæt ge on earum spræcu(n) . . . bið *on* hrofum bodud: quod in aurem locuti estis . . . praedicabitur in tectis.

Mt. 21: 5: þin cyning . . . rít *uppan* tamre assene: rex tuus . . . sedens super asina(m).

Mk. 11: 2: *ofer* þæne nán man gyt ne sæt: super quem nemo athuc hominum sedit.

Lk. 19: 30: *on* þa(m) nan man gyt ne sæt : cui nemo umquam hominum sedit.

Jn. 12: 14: se hælend . . . rad *on-uppan* þa(m): i(esu)s . . . sedit super eum.

Jn. 12: 15: þin cing cymþ *uppan* assan folan sittende : rex tuus uenit sedens super pullum ásine.

Mt. 21: 7: [hi] lédon hyra reaf *uppan* hig. (and) setton hyne *an-uppan* : inposuerunt super eis uestimenta sua et eum desuper sedere fecerunt.

Mk. 11: 7: hi hyra reaf *on* á-ledon (and) he *on* sæt: inponunt illi uestimenta sua et sedit super eum.

Lk. 19: 35: hig ... hyra reaf wurpon *ofer* þæne folan. (and) þæne hælend *on-ufan* setton : iactantes uestimenta sua supra pullum inposuerunt i(esu)m.

Mt. 21: 44: seþe fylþ *uppan* þysne stan : qui ceciderit super lapidem istum.

Lk. 20: 18: þe fylþ *ofer* þæne stán: qui ceciderit supra illum lapide(m).

Mt. 21: 44: ðe he *onuppan* fylð: super quem . . . ceciderit.

Lk. 20: 18: *ofer* þæne þe he fylð: supra quem autem ceciderit.

Mt. 23: 4: Hig . . . lecgeað þa *uppan* manna exla: inponunt in umeros hominum.

Mt. 24: 2: ne bið her læfed stan *uppan* stane: non relinquetur hic lapis super lapidem.

Mk. 13: 2: ne bið her læfed stan *ofer* stan: non relinquetur lapis super lapidem.

Lk. 19: 44: hig ne læfað on þe stán *ofer* stáne: non relinquent in té lapidem super lapide(m).

Lk. 21: 6: ne bið stan læfed *ofer* stan : non relinquetur lapis super lapidem.

Mt. 24: 3: he sæt *uppan* oliuetes dune : Sedente . . . eo sup(er) montem oliueti.

Mk. 13: 3: hi sæton *on* oliuetes dúne: sederet in monte(m) oliuarum.

Mt. 24: 17: seþe ys *uppan* hys huse: qui in tecto.

Mk. 13: 15: se ðe is *ofer* þécene: qui super tec[t]um.

Lk. 17: 31: se ðe bið *on* þécene: qui fuerint in tecto.

Mt. 26: 7: seo . . . agéat *uppan* hys heafud : effudit super caput ipsius.

Mk. 14: 3: an wif . . . *ofer* his heafod agét: mulier . . . effudit super caput eius.

Mt. 26: 30: þa ferdon hig *uppan* oliuetes dune: exierunt in montem oliueti.

Mk. 14: 26: hi ferdon *on* ele-bergena munt : exierunt in montem oliuarum.

Lk. 22: 39: he ut-eode *on* þæne munt oliuarum þ(æt) ys elebergena: egressus ibat . . . in montem oliuarum.

Jn. 6: 15: þa fleah he ana *uppon* þone munt: Fugit iterum in monte ipse solus.

Mt. 28: 2: drihtenes engel . . . awylte þone stan (and) sæt þær *on-uppan*: angelus . . . d(omi)ni . . . reuoluit lapidem et sedebat super eum.

Jn. 11: 38: þar wæs an stán *on-uppan* g(e)led: lapis superpositus erat ei.

Jn. 6: 19: þa gesawon hig þone hælend *uppan* þære sæ gán: uident i(esu)m ambulante(m) super mare.

Jn. 20: 7: þ(æt) swat-lin þe wæs *uppan* his heafde: sudarium quod fuerat supra capud eius.

It should be remarked that Matthew and John have also

ofer and *on*; but the introduction of *uppan* (*on-uppan*) as synonymous with *on* and *ofer* marks a fundamental difference in the vocabularies of Matthew and John as contrasted with Mark and Luke. The difference is doubtless due to locality rather than to time; for Alfred (sparingly) and Ælfric (profusely) use *uppan* (*on-uppan*) in the sense of *on* or *ofer* (see especially Sw. Alf. C. P., pp. 397: 34; 399: 2, 4, 6, 10, consulting the Latin original; and see Ælfric passim, but particularly Grein's Ælf., Gen. 50: 1; Ex. 4: 9).

The "restoration" of the last seven verses of Mark in the Royal MS. betrays its spurious character by the introduction of *uppen* (Mk. 16: 18) in place of *ofer* in the Corpus MS.*

xii. TRADO: BELÆWAN, (GE)SYLLAN.

If the proof of the composite authorship of the West Saxon Gospels depended solely upon the evidence of the varying translation of *trado*, the proof would still be amply sustained. Throughout Matthew and John, whenever *trado* describes a manifestly treacherous action, *belæwan* is used in the translation. This is not the case in Mark and Luke, which regularly have (*ge*)*syllan* instead of *belæwan*. The only occurrence of *belæwan* in these two Gospels is in Mk. 14: 10, where the Latin has *prodo*. It is remarkable that the Lindisfarne and Rushworth texts have *belæwan* in the same passage and there only. The fragments of the Gothic Gospels in representing the Greek παραδίδωμι agree almost without exception with the usage in the West Saxon Matthew and John, and show us what we should expect from a single translator of the Gospels. Of course, the fact that John agrees with Matthew does not necessarily mean that these two Gospels are by the same translator; but that Mark and Luke should differ so systematically from Matthew and John can scarcely admit of more than one interpretation. Let the reader examine and judge for himself.

Mt. 4: 12: þa se hæland gehyrde þ(æt) iohannes *belæwed* wæs: Cum . . . audisset quod iohannes traditus esset.

---

*Another interesting feature of this restoration is the appearance of *ge-funted* for *gefullod*.

Mk. 1: 14: Syððan iohannes *gesealde* wæs: Postquam autem traditus est iohannes.

Gothic Mk. 1: 14: Iþ afar þatei atgibans varþ Iohannes.

Mt. 10: 4: Iudas scarioth þe hyne *belæwde*: iudas scariotes qui et tradidit eum.

Mt. 26: 25: iudas þe hyne *be-læwde*: iudas qui tradidit eum.

Mt. 27: 3: iudas þe hyne *belæwde*: iudas qui eum tradidit.

Gothic Mt. 27: 3: Iudas sa *galevjands* ina.

Jn. 6: 71: be iuda scariobe þes hine *belæwde*: iudam simonis scariothis hic enim erat traditurus eum.

Gothic Jn. 6: 71: þana Iudan Seimonis, Iskariotu, sa auk habaida ina *galevjan*.

Jn. 12: 4: iudas scarioð þe hine *belæwde*: iudas scariotis qui erat eum traditur(u)s.

Gothic Jn. 12: 4: Judas Seimonis sa Iskariotes, izei skaftida sik du *galevjan* ina.

Jn. 18: 2: Iudas þe hyne *belæwde*: iudas qui tradebat eum.

Gothic Jn. 18: 2: Iudas sa *galevjands* ina.

Jn. 18: 5: iudas þe hine *belæwde*: iudas qui tradebat eum.

Gothic Jn. 18: 5: Iudas sa *levjands* ina.

Mt. 10: 19: Þon(ne) *belæwaþ syllað* eow: Cum autem tradent uos.

Mk. 13: 11: þon(ne) hi *syllende* eow læþað: cum duxerint uos tradentes.

Mt. 24: 10: manega . . . *belæwað* betwyx him: multi . . . inuicem tradent.

Mt. 26: 15: ic hyne *belæwe* eow: ego uobis eum trada(m).

Mk. 14: 10: þ(æt) he hine *belæwde*: ut proderet eum.

Gothic Mk. 14: 10: ei *galevidedi* ina.

Lk. 22: 4: hu he hine hi(m) *gesealde*: quem-ammodum illu(m) traderet eis.

Mt. 26: 16: þ(æt) he hyne wolde *belewan*: ut eum traderet.

Mk. 14: 11: hu he hine digellice *sealde*: quomodo illum oportune traderet.
Gothic Mk. 14: 11: hvaiva gatilaba ina *galevidedi*.
Lk. 22: 6: hu he eaðelicust hine . . . *gesealde*: ut traderet illum.
Mt. 26: 21: án eower *belæwð* me: unus uestrum me traditurus est.
Mt. 26: 23: Seþe be-dypð on disce mid me hys hand se me *be-læwð*: qui intingit mecum manum in parapside hic me tradet.
Mk. 14: 18: eower án þe mid me yt *gesylð* me: unus ex uobis me tradet qui manducat mecum.
Lk. 22: 21: her is þæs *læwan* hand mid me on mysan : ecce manus tradentis me mecum est in mensa.
Mt. 26: 24: þurh þone þe byþ mannes sunu *be-læwed*: per quem filius hominis traditur.
Mk. 14: 21: þurh þone þe mannes sunu *geseald* bið: per quem filius hominis traditur.
Lk. 22: 22: þe he þurh *geseald* bið: per quem tradetur.
Mt. 26: 46. nu genealæcð se þe me *be-læwð*: appropinquauit qui me tradit.
Mk. 14: 42: nu is gehende se ðe me *sylð*: ecce qui me tradit prope est.
Gothic Mk. 14: 42: Sai, sa levjands mik atnehvida.
Mt. 26: 48: Se þe hyne *be-læwde* sealde heo(m) tacn: Qui autem tradidit eum dedit illis signum.
Mt. 27: 1: þ(æt) hig hyne deaþe *be-læwdon*: ut eum morti traderent.
Gothic Mt. 27: 1: ei afdauþidedeina ina: ὥστε θανατῶσαι αὐτόν.
Lk. 22: 48: mannes sunu þu mid cosse *sylst*: osculo filium hominis tradis ?
Jn. 6: 64: hwa hine *belæwon* wolde : quis traditurus esset eum.
Gothic Jn. 6: 64: hvas ist saei galeiveiþ ina.
Jn. 13: 2: þ(æt) he hine *belæwde*: ut traderet eum.
Jn. 13: 11: he wiste witodlice hwa hyne sceolde *belæwan*: sciebat enim quis-nam esset qui traderet eum.

Jn. 21: 20: Drihten. hwæt ys se ðe belæwð: d(omi)ne quis est qui tradit te?*

With *belæwan* we close the argument. The consistent and persistent testimony of this word carries conviction with its weight, and satisfies the true spirit of inquiry. If, however, the curious reader would investigate this subject still further, he may be interested in the translations of *amen (amen)dico, festuca, hymno dicto, latro, nubes, phantasma, purpura, spelunca latronum, sub modio, terrae motus,* etc., etc.; though doubtless many of these variations ought to be regarded as allowable to a single translator. The use of *to hwi* six times in Matthew and not once in the other three Gospels may be of interest, particularly as the phrase is unusual in Anglo-Saxon.

It may be queried whether in the course of this search any facts have been discovered, which tend to militate against the separation of the Gospels, on the basis of a supposed plurality of authorship, into the groups—Matthew—Mark and Luke—John.

---

* *Trado* occurs elsewhere as follows:

Mt. 5: 25; 10: 17, 21; 11: 27; 17: 22; 18: 34; 20: 18, 19; 24: 9, 38; 25: 14, 20, 22; 26: 2, 45, 59; 27: 2, 4, 18, 26.
Mk. 3: 19; 7: 4, 13; 9: 31; 10: 33, 33; 13: 9, 12; 14: 41, 55; 15: 1, 10, 15.
Lk. 1: 2; 4: 6, 17; 9: 44; 10: 22; 12: 58; 18: 32; 20: 20, 34; 21: 12, 12, 16; 23: 25; 24: 7, 20.
Jn. 18: 30, 35, 36; 19: 11, 16, 30.
The Gothic translates $\pi\alpha\rho\alpha\delta i\delta\omega\mu\iota$ in the following unquoted passages:
Mt. 5: 25; 26: 2; 27; 2, 4, 18.
Mk. 7: 13; 9: 31; 10: 33; 14: 41; 15: 1, 10, 15.
Lk. 1: 2; 4: 6; 9: 44; 10: 22; 18: 32; 20: 20.
Jn. 18: 30, 35, 36; 19: 11.

In these passages (except as noted below), the context does not show that *trado* ($\pi\alpha\rho\alpha\delta i\delta\omega\mu\iota$) is to be taken in the sense of *to betray*. The usage of the West Saxon Matthew and John in rendering these passages differs from that of the Gothic in the same passages (or in the parallel passages in Mark and Luke) only in Mt. 26: 45 (Gothic Mk. 14: 41); Mt. 27: 4; Jn. 18: 36; 19: 11; where the Gothic is doubtless wrong in Mk. 14: 41, as is indicated by the Gothic in Mk. 9: 31; 10: 33; Lk. 9: 44. The Gothic is evidently wrong in Jn. 18: 36. In Mt. 27: 4; Jn. 19: 11, the West Saxon version has probably deviated from the rule otherwise observed.

The reply is that nothing of moment has presented itself, but see Mt. 7: 15; 10: 17; 16: 6, 12; Mk. 8: 15; 12: 38; Lk. 12: 1, 15; 20: 46; Rush. Mt. 16: 12; also Mt. 17; 3; Mk. 9: 14; Lk. 9: 30; 22: 4. It may be added that the orthography of the Corpus text of Mark is peculiar in never having *hig* for *hi*, *hyne* for *hine*, *hym* for *him*, or *-un* for *-on* as a termination of a verb; etc., etc. The Corpus scribe has doubtless been consistent and accurate. The contrast between Mark on the one hand and Matthew, Luke, and John on the other is explainable by supposing the introduction of a "different hand" in Mark in some ancestral MS.

Résumé.—By way of recapitulation, we have seen that in the West Saxon version of the Gospels

A. Matthew is separated from the three other Gospels
   (a) By the use (limited) of the weak form of *heofon*.
   (b) By the use (limited) of *underfon* synonymously with *onfon*.
   (c) By the use (occasional) of *willan* after þæt introducing past purpose.
   (d) By the use (regular) of þæra, þær, hwær, instead of þara, þar, hwar.
B. Matthew is separated from Mark and Luke
   (e) By the use of *hundredes ealdor* instead of *hundredman*.
C. Matthew is separated from Luke
   (f) By the use of *ligyt* instead of *ligræsc*.
   (g) By the use of *gristbitung* instead of *grystlung*.
D. John is separated from the other gospels
   (h) By the use (regular) of the plural of *heofon* where the singular should be expected.
   (i) By the use of *underfon* almost to the exclusion of *onfon*.
   (j) By the use (excessive) of *willan* after þæt, introducing past purpose.
   (k) By the use of þara and þæra, þar and þær, hwar and hwær, interchangeably.
E. Matthew and John are separated from Mark and Luke
   (l) By the frequent use of *witodlice* in translating *autem*.
   (m) By the use of *cocc* instead of *hana*.

(n) By the use (frequent) of *uppan* (*on-uppan*) with loss of the original force of *upp-*.

(o) By the correct translation of *vox clamantis*.

(p) By the use of *belæwan* instead of (*ge*)*syllan* in translating *trado* where the notion of treachery is indicated by the context.

Finally, in the evidence presented we have seen weighty reasons for believing that the authorship of the West Saxon Gospels is at least dual, and probably triple; more explicitly, that the Matthew is by one translator, the Mark and Luke by another, the John by a third (unless possibly by the translator of the Matthew); that the translator of the Matthew and the translator of the John were probably locally akin, possibly translating conjointly; and that the translator of the Mark and Luke was probably distant from the locality where the Matthew and the John were translated. Furthermore, in view of the agreement of the Northumbrian version with the West Saxon Mark and Luke in the exclusion of *underfon* (except Lind. Jn. 4: 45, as noted), in the use of *hana* instead of *cocc*, in the exclusion of *uppan* (*on-uppan*) in the sense of *on* or *ofer*, and in the solitary employment of *belæwan* (Mk. 14: 10 *prodo*), it seems not unlikely that the Northumbrian version (and the Old Mercian Matthew?) and the West Saxon Mark and Luke are in somewise akin, probably as respects localities of translation. The importance of the fact that these versions agree in the use of (*ge*)*syllan* to translate *trado* and of *belæwan* to translate *prodo*, is emphasized by the consideration that "In those days, when grammars and dictionaries were hardly known or used, Latin was studied much more as a living language than it is now" (cf. Sw. Alf. C. P., p. xli).

www.ingramcontent.com/pod-product-compliance
Lightning Source LLC
Chambersburg PA
CBHW030709110426
42739CB00031B/1519